Extreme Sports

MICHAEL DEAN

Level 2

Series Editors: Andy Hopkins and Jocelyn Potter

Pearson Education Limited
Edinburgh Gate, Harlow,
Essex CM20 2JE, England
and Associated Companies throughout the world.

ISBN: 978-1-4058-8159-3

First published by Penguin Books Ltd 2001
This edition published 2008

1 3 5 7 9 10 8 6 4 2

Typeset by Graphicraft Ltd, Hong Kong
Set in 11/14pt Rotis Serif
Printed in China
SWTC/01

Published by Pearson Education Ltd in association with
Penguin Books Ltd, both companies being subsidiaries of Pearson Plc

Acknowledgements
All Sport: p.5; www.moyes.com.au: pp.6 and 7; Press Association: p.9; John Cleare: p.14;
Stock Shot: pp.16 and 18; Stockfile: p.20; Associated Press: pp.21 and 22; Frank Spooner: p.23;
Alexander Photography: p.24.

Contents

Introduction iv

What Are Extreme Sports?
Are extreme sports for you? 1
A–Z of extreme sports 2

Up in the Air
Call the police! It's BASE jumping 4
Bill Moyes—the father of hang gliding 6
Skydiving stories 8

Down on the Ground
Love goes down—street luge 10
It started with Wendy—snowboarding 13

Under the Water
I did cave diving (and lived) 15
What's new this week?—canyoning 18

Games and Races
The X Games 20
Extreme sports races 21
Extreme sports team races 24

What Do You Know Now about Extreme Sports? 25

Answers 26

Activities 27

Introduction

When people ask, "Why do people do extreme sports?" this is your answer: "Michael Bane was afraid of high places. But then he went up a mountain and raced down that mountain on a bike. Now he has no problem with high places. That's why."

This book is about extreme sports. The sports are all very different. Some start in the air—BASE jumping, hang gliding, and skydiving. Some are on the ground—street luge and snowboarding. Some are under the water—cave diving and canyoning.

This is also a book about people. Phil Smith of Houston, Texas, is BASE 1—the first BASE jumper. Bill Moyes from Australia is th father of hang gliding. He is the father of a big family, too, and they are *all* hang gliders. And we meet the US Extreme Sports Team; they snowboarded down the biggest mountain in Antarctica. John and Shelley Orlowski married underwater in Mexico. Dave Mirra is the greatest BMX bike champion in extreme sport. Michael Bane did thirteen extreme sports races in one year.

And I, Michael Dean, the writer of this book, did cave diving for the first time in Florida. You can read about it here. Before that trip, I only went underwater in my bath.

What Are Extreme Sports?

Are extreme sports for you?

Answer these questions. Then you will know.

1 You are high on a mountain. You look down. What do you feel?
a I want to go down—NOW!
b I like it up here.
c I want to go higher and look down again.

2 You are on a mountain. You are climbing and it's easy. Then it snows. Now it's dangerous. What are you going to do?
a I'll wait. The snow will stop—I hope!
b I'm going down.
c I'll start skiing.

3 You can have a bike for your birthday. What do you want?
a I want a very slow bike with three wheels.
b I want a fast bike.
c I want a BMX bike. I want to do tricks on it.

4 You are driving a car. You can go fast on this road and there are no other cars on it. How fast do you go?
a I always drive slowly.
b Fast, but not very fast.
c Very fast—but I also drive well.

5 You go to a pool every week. What do you do there?
a I have a coffee and watch my friends in the pool.
b I swim slowly up and down the pool.
c I swim under the water for as long as I can.

What do your answers mean? Look at page 26.

A – Z of extreme sports

There are a lot of extreme sports. Here is an A–Z of some of them. Write 0–10 in the box on the right.
0 = This sport is not for me!
10 = This sport is great. I really want to try it.

aerial ballet . . . .

You jump out of an airplane with some friends. Before your parachute opens, you dance with them in the sky.

aggressive in-line skating . . . .

You jump up high on your skates. You kick and you do tricks.

BASE jumping . . . .

You jump off a building or a bridge with a parachute. You usually open your parachute as late as possible.

BMX bike riding (vert) . . . .

There are three kinds of BMX bike riding. In vert, you do as many tricks as you can in one minute.

canyoning . . . .

Bungee jumping is a jump from a high place with a rope around you. Canyoning is the same—but into cold water!

cave diving . . . .
You dive under the water with air on your back.

hang gliding . . . .
This is the oldest extreme sport. Otto Lillienthal, a German, did it in 1893.

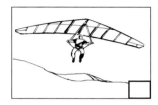

snowboarding . . . .
Snowboarders do tricks on their snowboards in the snow.

street luge . . . .
The board has wheels on it. You get on the board, on your back, and go down the road at about 110 kph.*

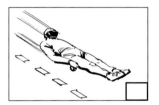

wakeboarding . . . .
A boat pulls you and your board over the water—fast. You do tricks on your board.

zorbing . . . .
You climb into a three-meter ball. Then somebody pushes the ball down the street at about 50 kph.

kph: kilometers in an hour

Up in the Air

Call the police!
It's BASE jumping

What's the most dangerous extreme sport? Maybe it's BASE jumping. In the US, the police put BASE jumpers in prison. Go to France, Norway, or Brazil—you can jump there. John Vincent of New Orleans went to prison for ninety days after a jump. He jumped from a tall building in St. Louis. The police were there when he came down.

BASE jumping started at El Capitan, a 915-meter-high mountain in Yosemite, an American park. In 1978, some people jumped from the mountain with parachutes. People BASE jump there today, too.

In 1981, Phil Smith and Jean Boenisch started the US BASE Association. You have to do 100 skydives and then you get a BASE number. Phil Smith of Houston, Texas, is BASE 1.

Some people BASE jump from 76-meter buildings. That isn't very high! You have to open your parachute very quickly after you jump. You have to fall well and watch the ground. Are there people there? Turn your parachute and move away. Quickly—you don't have much time. And are the police there . . . ?

Why do people do BASE jumping? Because the world is beautiful when you see it from above. And because it's dangerous. About one person each year dies after a jump. BASE jumper Rick Harrison broke his legs on a jump. He shows you his legs and tells you about it. Then he finds a building or a bridge and jumps again.

More people are jumping every year. Who will be the next person in the BASE Association? You?

A BASE jumper above a city

Bill Moyes — the father of hang gliding

Australian Bill Moyes was thirty-four when he started hang gliding. That's old for an extreme sport! When his son Steve was fourteen, Bill woke him up at four o'clock every morning. They went hang gliding before Steve went to school. Later Steve was a world champion, and there's a movie about Bill and Steve, *The Birdmen of Kilimanjaro*. The father and son climbed up to the top of the mountain and flew down to the bottom.

Bill Moyes

Flying was Bill Moyes's life. He loved to fly, but he didn't like airplanes. In 1966, he flew higher than any man in the world, at 350 meters above the ground. In 1970, he stopped jumping off mountains. Airplanes pulled his hang glider through the sky. In 1971, he flew at 2,866 meters.

Bill Moyes started to make and sell hang gliders. He sold his first hang glider in 1967. He was very happy—and he took the man home for dinner! His son Steve and his daughter Vicki worked with him. They made the Xtralite, the world's number one hang glider. Bill hang glided ten or twelve times every year because he wanted to try his new hang gliders.

When Bill Moyes looks back on his life, is he happy? "I wanted to do these things and I did them," Bill told *Hang Gliding* magazine. "It wasn't difficult."

Masters of

Grandfathe

Steve Moyes was a hang gliding world champion.

"HE DIED FOR ME"
Michael Costello's story

Skydive Orlando, at Umatilla, Florida, is famous for skydiving. World champions jump from airplanes here and skydive down through the sky. They fall . . . and fall . . . Then they open their parachutes at the last minute.

But Gareth Griffiths from Britain wasn't a world champion skydiver. It was his first visit to Florida and his first skydive. He paid $200 for it. Five friends from Britain watched him from the little airport. They watched Gareth go up in the airplane with his American instructor, Michael Costello.

At 4,000 meters, Michael and Gareth jumped. Gareth was on Michael's back and the parachute was on Gareth's back. They fell to 1,500 meters. All skydivers know that the fall through the sky is beautiful. But at 1,500 meters, Gareth's parachute didn't open. He and Michael fell fast. Gareth's friends at the airport watched and were afraid for him.

For Michael Costello this was one of more than 8,000 skydives in his life. Three thousand of those dives were with a "new boy" on his back. But Gareth had the parachute, and the parachute wasn't open. Michael couldn't do anything about it.

Michael took Gareth's arms in his hands and pulled him around. Now Michael was under Gareth. Michael hit the ground first and he died. Gareth was on top of Michael and he lived.

When the parachute didn't open, one of them had to die. Michael knew that. He died for Gareth.

"I THOUGHT, 'I'M DEAD ...'"
Bren Jones's story

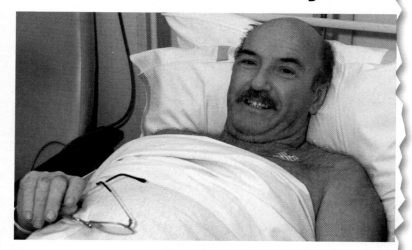

Bren Jones is a parachute instructor and he really enjoys aerial ballet. This was a good day for him. It was an aerial ballet and one more of the 3,500 parachute jumps in his life.

Four men jumped from the airplane. They did a beautiful aerial ballet high in the blue sky, at 1,800 meters. Then they opened their parachutes and started to fall at 193 kph. But Bren's parachute hit the parachute of his friend Eddie.

All skydivers have two parachutes, and Eddie opened his second parachute. He came down. But Eddie's first parachute was on Bren's parachute and Bren's parachute closed again. He fell fast with two closed parachutes on his back.

At 120 meters, Bren tried to open his second parachute. It didn't open but it made his fall slower. He fell at only 40 kph. And then he hit the ground, feet first.

He opened his eyes in hospital. "At first I thought, 'I'm dead'," Bren said later. Then I said, "I'll stay here, in this bed." And the doctor said, "Yes, don't jump out."

Today Bren is fine.

Down on the Ground

Love goes down — street luge

Look at that! Watch them go down!

I want to do that, but in the street. Street luge!

Joe buys a board, clothes, and shoes for street luge.

Joe, no! It's dangerous!

Great!

113 kph down a street near Joe's home.

12

It started with Wendy — snowboarding

In 1965, the Poppen family were at home in Michigan, US. It was winter and there was snow and ice on the ground. Sherman Poppen watched his daughter go down the ice on some wood. Wendy tried to stand up on the wood, but she couldn't. She fell every time. Sherman had an idea. He went into his garage and made a board. Now we call it a snowboard. That same day, Wendy's friends wanted boards, too.

Snowboarding is good on hard snow and ice. But you can use today's boards on wet snow, too. Extreme snowboarders go down dangerous mountains. They can turn right, turn left . . . They can go to beautiful places. Only snowboarders and mountain animals see these places.

But in the 1980s, there was a problem. Skiers didn't want the snowboarders on the mountains. Skiers start at the top of a mountain and then go down. Snowboarders go across the mountain, in front of the skiers. But skiers slowly understood the snowboarders' love for the mountains. Now more and more people go snowboarding.

Crested Butte is a beautiful mountain town in Colorado. In 1997, it was the first extreme sports center in the US for snowboarding. In 1998, the Winter X Games were there and snowboarding was one of the games. Now there are snowboarding parks, too. Snowboarders can jump and do tricks on the snow.

Thirty-five years after Wendy Poppen went down the ice in Michigan, the United States Extreme Sports Team had an idea. They wanted to climb the highest mountain in Antarctica and snowboard down the ice. Mount Vincent is almost 5,000 meters high and it's the coldest mountain in the world.

Mount Vincent—the world's coldest mountain

Here's Doug Stoup, of the US Extreme Sports Team. The trip was his idea.

"Antarctica is very cold. It's −20°C when there's no sun. But when the sun comes out, it's hot! Crazy!"

On the mountain, the team tried to sleep as much as possible.

"When you're very high, you get tired. You have to drink a lot of water and eat a lot of food. It doesn't stop snowing here. We're having the worst snow and wind for a hundred years! It's wet snow, good for snowboarding. There's no night here, only 24-hour days. It's light all the time. The hottest time of the day is from four in the afternoon to midnight. I'm learning to sleep by day or night."

The team climbed to the top of Mount Vincent in December 1999. The weather was good and they snowboarded down the mountain.

Under the Water

I did cave diving (and lived)

My name's Michael Dean. I'm writing this book for you. These extreme sports are exciting and I love writing about them. But I wanted to do one, too. I wanted to do a *new* extreme sport—new to me. So I did! I did cave diving for the first time.

Before you can dive, you have to get a C-card. This card says that you can dive underwater with air on your back. That wasn't difficult. I found an instructor. I started to dive. I got a C-card.

"Where do you want to go diving?" my instructor asked me, when I had the C-card.

"Florida," I said. "I want to dive in caves."

"That's dangerous," he said. "One mistake and you die."

So I asked a cave diver, not a C-card instructor.

"Is cave diving dangerous?" I asked John Orlowski.

Orlowski and his wife Shelley are the most famous cave divers in the world. They married underwater in a cave in Mexico.

"Cave diving isn't more dangerous than other diving," said Orlowski, "when the diver has a good instructor and good equipment."

So equipment was the next problem. Diving is an expensive sport. But I bought the equipment. I was ready.

Madison Cave, in Florida, is a very big cave. In big caves, the instructors put lines in the water. Each line is a different color. The lines stay there all the time and they help the divers. In smaller caves, each diver puts down a line so he or she can get back again.

So this is it. It's the day of my first cave dive, and I have almost 100 kilos of diving equipment on my back. My instructor's name is Kirk. The water in Madison Cave is warm (about 22°C) all year, and it's blue. The cave is dark and quiet and very beautiful. So how do I feel? Afraid!

Cave diving in Florida

I have the line in my hand. On their first cave dive, divers often have the line in their hand all the time. I can see Kirk's light in front of me. Then, suddenly, I don't see it. Where is he? I want to shout, but I can't. I'm very afraid.

I see his light to the right. He left the blue line and went into another cave! Do I follow him? What did my cave diving instructors say about this? I want to shout Kirk's name. But I can't because we're ten meters down under the water. I have the blue line in my left hand. I stop and wait.

I do nothing for two minutes. It's the longest two minutes of my life. I have an idea. I have an underwater pen, so I can write to Kirk. I can write, "I'm going back up." Then, I can leave it on the line.

Kirk comes behind me. I can see his mouth. He's smiling and saying, "Hello." He writes something for me.

"Michael," he writes, "you did the right thing." I smile.

Sometimes people go down into a cave and they don't come up again. So a cave diver never forgets two things. One: Don't leave the line! Two: Don't follow—think!

On my next dive into the Madison, there's a young diver from England with Kirk and me. Her name's Sally and this is her first cave dive.

We follow the line without light. You have to learn that. And then we swim with only half our air. Later, we go to the smaller caves. There's no line. We swim for about eight meters with no air because that's important for a diver. Sometimes you have no air and you have to get up quickly. Down there in the dark, eight meters is a very long time!

We swim back to the line. Kirk pulls the line. *OK?* he's saying. I pull the line: *OK*. Sally pulls the line and we go slowly back. But then the water behind me moves. Sally is away from the line, but she has her hand on my leg. She pulls my leg. Then she pulls the equipment on my back.

Oh no! I'm shouting in my head. *Get your hand off my air. I don't want to die.* I'm shouting, but I'm also turning. I'm trying to help her. Kirk swims under her and pushes her up to the line. She takes the line in her hand and pulls: *OK*.

That evening, we sit in the warm Florida air and drink coffee.

"Do you like cave diving?" Kirk asks me.

"Yes, I do."

"Do you want to do it again, after you finish the book?" asks Sally.

"Oh yes!"

What's new this week?— canyoning

There's something new in extreme sports every year—no, every week! Sometimes the new sport starts from an old sport. First there was bungee jumping. Now people do canyoning.

A canyoning jump

When you bungee jump, you jump from a mountain, from a building, or from a bridge. You have a rope around you. Bungee jumping started in New Zealand and the magazine *National Geographic* wrote about it in 1955. Now 10,000,000 people can say, "I did a bungee jump." The highest bungee jump was 180 meters from a building in Auckland, New Zealand.

When you do canyoning, you also jump with a rope around you. But you fall down and down and down . . . into very cold water. The sport started in France, and it's dangerous.

In the past, you could go on canyoning vacations in Europe. You paid for two weeks in Switzerland, and you did a lot of jumps. Now, it's more difficult. There aren't as many companies as before. One Swiss company stopped their canyoning vacations when somebody died.

A seventeen-year-old British girl died canyoning in the Blue Mountains near Sydney, Australia. There was no instructor there. She had a rope but no other equipment. The jump was her first time at an extreme sport. The Blue Mountains are beautiful but there's no town there. It was five hours before people found her.

In one year, twenty-one people died. "People are jumping into water head first from places thirty meters high," says extreme sports instructor Phil Maguire. "Sometimes they hit their heads when they go in. And they're jumping into 300 meters of water. Sometimes the water is moving very fast. Some people don't come up again."

BASE jumping is dangerous, too, of course, but there's a US BASE Association. The association helps people. There's no canyoning association. There are only young people with no equipment and no instructor.

So what's the answer? Do we stop this extreme sport in beautiful mountains? In some places in the US, you can go to prison for canyoning. But there are some good vacation companies in Switzerland, Austria, France, and Germany. They have instructors and equipment, and they do other mountain sports, too.

Games and Races
The X Games

Every year in the US there's a summer X Games (Extreme Sports Games) and a winter X Games. The first summer X Games was in 1995 in Rhode Island. The winter X Games started two years later with mountain biking on snow, ice climbing, and other games. Now there's an Asian X Games, an Australian X Games, a European X Games, an X Games for young people . . . There are ten X Games around the world.

Dave Mirra, the world's number one BMX rider, was the BMX vert champion. Dave started to do tricks on a bike when he was thirteen or fourteen. He did five hours of tricks every day. He was in his first extreme sports race when he was fourteen. Dave was a champion nine times in six X Games. There's a movie about Dave and X Games champion Ryan Nyquist— *Miracle Boy and Nyquist*. And you can do Dave's tricks on a computer game—*Dave Mirra BMX*. It really is Dave—Sony filmed his tricks for the game.

Dave Mirra

And who is the women's extreme sports champion? Maybe the beautiful Mehgan Heaney-Greer from the US diving team. At twenty-one, she can go under the water to fifty-five meters with no air. She stays down there for two minutes and loves it.

Extreme sports races

Close your eyes and think of an extreme sportsman. What did you see? Was he about twenty years old? A big man? That's not Michael Bane.

Michael Bane was forty-six when he started extreme sports. He was fat. He didn't walk to work. But his friend did snowboarding, and one day Michael went with him. Michael was afraid and he fell off the board. When he got home, he was sick. But it was the best day of his life.

Michael had an idea. He wanted to be in the most dangerous extreme sports races in the US. He wanted to do thirteen of them in one year. There were two big problems. Michael couldn't swim, and he was afraid of high places. But he learned to swim. (The other people in the class were all children.) And he went higher and higher in the mountains.

Michael wrote a book, *Over the Edge*, about his extreme sports races. Here are three of the races in the book.

The Swim from Alcatraz

Alcatraz was a prison in the water near San Francisco. Now, every fall, people swim from there to San Francisco. It's about three kilometers. Two hundred and fifty people are doing it this year and Michael is one of them.

There's one small problem: the water between Alcatraz and San Francisco is very cold. There's a bigger problem, too. The water has sharks in it.

Swimmers finish the race from Alcatraz

The Death Valley Race

Everybody runs. People run for a bus. That isn't an extreme sport. But some people run 230 kilometers across Death Valley and then up the highest mountain in the US. *That's* an extreme sport.

Death Valley is in California. It's very hot (51°C in the summer) and very dry. The Death Valley Race is in July, the hottest time of the year. It starts at Badwater and goes up Mount Whitney, 4,417 meters high. People carry water for the racers, so nobody dies.

Michael ran all 230 kilometers.

Death Valley Race, California

The Kamikaze* Bike Race

This is the most dangerous bike race in the world. You go down a mountain very fast on a bike. But Michael didn't have a bike. He bought one from a friend for $100. Then he went down Mammoth Mountain, California, on it.

Before he started, Michael asked an instructor, "After I start, can I stop?" The answer was, "No, you can't. You'll die."

Michael Bane and the other people in the race went down at 72 kph. Michael didn't stop. He didn't die. And now he isn't afraid.

When people ask, "Why do people do extreme sports?" this is your answer: "Michael Bane was afraid of high places. But then he went up a mountain and raced down that mountain on a bike. Now he has no problem with high places. That's why."

The Kamikaze Downhill Bike Race

* kamikaze: in 1945, Japanese "kamikaze" airmen flew their airplanes into American ships and died.

Extreme sports team races

Britain's Mark Burnett started extreme sports team races in 1995. The first race was in Utah, in the US. Teams of five people raced 600 kilometers in ten days by mountain bike, by boat, and on foot.

But this race is different every year. One year, the teams had four people in them, and they had to get out of some difficult places in Borneo, Asia. They had to climb, and they also went hundreds of kilometers across the Pacific Ocean by boat.

All of this was on television. Not everybody likes that. Some people say that TV is the boss in extreme sports. American Don Mann started "The Beast" in May 2000. The race isn't on television and there are no expensive boats on the Pacific. The team walks 480 kilometers across Alaska, one of the coldest places in the world. And each person on the team pays $7,500 for the trip!

"The Beast"

What Do You Know Now about Extreme Sports?

1 Which of these extreme sports uses wheels?
  a aerial ballet
  b aggressive in-line skating
  c BASE jumping

2 Which BASE jumper jumped from a tall building in St. Louis?

3 What is the name of Bill Moyes's son?

4 About how high are you when you do an aerial ballet?

5 How is street luge different from ice luge?

6 Which mountain did the US Extreme Sports Team climb in December 1999? Where is it?

7 Where is a good place in the US for cave diving?

8 Which country did canyoning start in?

9 Where is Alcatraz?

10 Who was the greatest BMX bike champion?

The answers are on page 26.

ANSWERS

Are extreme sports for you?

What do your answers mean?
Are most of your answers a?
Are you in bed? Stay there, and don't get up. It's dangerous out there!
Are most of your answers b?
Think about the extreme sports in the book. Maybe one of them is for you.
Are most of your answers c?
Do you do extreme sports? No? Then start one. Extreme sports are for you!

What Do You Know Now About Extreme Sports?

1   b (aggressive in-line skating)
2   John Vincent
3   Steve Moyes
4   About 1,800 meters
5   Street luge is in the street and ice luge is on ice
6   Mount Vincent, in Antarctica
7   Madison Cave, Florida
8   France
9   In the water, near San Francisco
10   Dave Mirra

ACTIVITIES

Before you read

1 Read the Introduction. Look at the names of the extreme sports. How many of these do you know?

2 Look at the Word List at the back of the book. Find new words in your dictionary. Then answer these questions.

   a How many *extreme sports* can you name in your language?

   b Is a *champion* the best person or the worst person at a sport?

   c Does an *instructor* help you, or do you help him/her?

   d Do you fly or swim through the *air*?

   e Do you *dive* into or out of water?

   f Do you *ski* on snow or under water?

   g When you open a *parachute*, are you going up or down?

   h Do you wear *skates* on your hands or on your feet?

While you read

3 Where do these sports happen? Put a check (✓) in the right places.

	in the air	in/on water	on the ground
a aerial ballet	.....	.....	.....
b BASE jumping	.....	.....	.....
c bungee jumping	.....	.....	.....
d cave diving	.....	.....	.....
e hang gliding	.....	.....	.....
f snowboarding	.....	.....	.....
g street luge	.....	.....	.....
h wakeboarding	.....	.....	.....
i zorbing	.....	.....	.....

After you read

4 Talk to another student. Look at the *A–Z of extreme sports* again. Did you write the same numbers? Why (not)?

Pages 4–9

Before you read

5 Look at the picture on page 5. What is this person doing? What is on his
   or her back? Do you think this is dangerous? Do people go to prison for
   this in your country?

While you read

6 Who did what? Write the names in the right places.
   Phil Smith   Rick Harrison   Steve Moyes   Bill Moyes
   Michael Costello   Bren Jones
   a He hit the ground at 40 kph.   ....
   b He died for another man.   ....
   c He flew very high.   ....
   d He is BASE 1.   ....
   e He broke his legs.   ....
   f He was a world champion.   ....

After you read

7 How is BASE jumping different from a jump from an airplane? Which
   sport is more dangerous? Which is more exciting? Why? What do you
   think?

Pages 10–14

Before you read

8 You are going to read a story about Joe and Alma. Joe loves street luge.
   Alma isn't interested. What problems will they have, do you think?

While you read

9 Write the dates.
   1965   1980s   1998   1999
   a A team snowboarded down Mount Vincent.   ....
   b Skiers didn't want snowboarders on the mountains.   ....
   c Sherman Poppen made the first snowboard.   ....
   d The Winter X Games were in Crested Butte.   ....

After you read

10 Work with another student.

   Student A: You work for a newspaper. Ask Doug Stoup questions about his team's trip to Mount Vincent.

   Student B: You are Doug Stoup. Answer the questions.

Pages 15–19

Before you read

11 You can dive in the ocean, in a river, or in a cave. Which would you like to do? Which is most dangerous? Discuss this with another student.

While you read

12 In Michael's dive, what happened first? And then? Write the numbers 1–6.

   a He bought the equipment for cave diving.   .....
   b He couldn't see Kirk's light.   .....
   c He felt afraid in the water.   .....
   d He got a C-card.   .....
   e Kirk wrote something for him.   .....
   f He waited for two minutes on the blue line.   .....

After you read

13 You want to write a book about extreme sports. First, you want to try a sport. Which sport will you try? Why?

Pages 20–26

Before you read

14 What do you know about the X Games? Sometimes they are on TV. Look at the pictures on pages 20 and 21. What do you think X means? Discuss your ideas with another student.

While you read

15 Are these sentences right (✓) or wrong (✗)?

   a The X Games happen every four years.   .....
   b Michael Bane was fat when he started extreme sports.   .....
   c There are sharks in the water around Alcatraz.   .....

    d Michael Bane went down Mount Whitney on a bike.   .....

    e "The Beast" is a boat race across the Pacific.   .....

After you read

16 Where are/were these? Find the answers on the right.

a The first summer X Games.	Alaska
b A three-kilometer swim.	Death Valley
c A 230-kilometer run.	Mammoth Mountain
d A dangerous bike race.	Rhode Island
e A 600-kilometer race.	San Francisco
f A 480-kilometer race.	Utah

Writing

17 You are Otto Lilienthal. It is 1893. You are going to jump from a high place in your new hang-glider. Write about your feelings now.

18 "In the US, the police put BASE jumpers in prison." Do you think this is a good idea? Why (not)?

19 One of your friends is doing a very dangerous extreme sport. You don't like it. What do you say to them? Write your words.

20 Write a letter to Michael Bane. How do you feel about him? Tell him. Ask him some questions.

21 Write five questions for an instructor of one of the sports in this book. What do you want to know?

22 Which extreme sport would you like to try? Why?

WORD LIST *with example sentences*

air (n) There are not many cars in the country, so the *air* is cleaner.

association (n) The Football *Association* (FA) is English; there is a different association for Scottish football.

board (n) You stand on your *board* and the water carries you to the beach.

cave (n) Those animals live in *caves* in the mountains.

champion (n) Muhammad Ali is famous because he was a world *champion* three times.

dive (n/v) My first *dive* was in the Pacific Ocean and I saw some beautiful fish.

equipment (n) He wanted to climb the mountain with us, but he didn't have the right *equipment*.

extreme sport (n) I sit in an office all week, but on the weekend I enjoy *extreme sports* in exciting places.

instructor (n) There is an *instructor* at the pool, and he is giving me swimming lessons.

line (n) They are standing in *line* for tickets.
Take the other end of the *line* and put it around the tree.

parachute (n) After you jump from the airplane, you have to open your *parachute*!

prison (n) My father killed a man and went to *prison* for twenty years.

race (n/v) She won the 400 meter *race*, and the Japanese woman came second.

rope (n) When I climb mountains, I always use *ropes*.

shark (n) Sometimes *sharks* kill swimmers, but not very often.

skate (n) You can move fast with *skates* on your feet.

ski (v) There isn't much snow in the Alps this year, so we are going *skiing* in Canada.

team (n) They go to all their *team's* football games.

trick (n) Watch this *trick*! I can put my feet behind my head!

wheel (n) On some very old bikes, the front *wheel* was bigger than the back wheel.

The Whistle and Dead Men's Eyes

M. R. James

Two Englishmen go away for a quiet holiday. But it is not very quiet in one man's hotel room. Somebody – or something – is using the other bed. What is it and why is it angry? The other man sees things, but they are not really there. Or are they? What is happening? Read these ghost stories and be afraid. Be very afraid!

The Mummy

"Imhotep is half-dead and will be half-dead for all time."

The Mummy is an exciting movie. Imhotep dies in Ancient Egypt. 3,700 years later Rick O'Connell finds him. Imhotep is very dangerous. Can O'Connell send him back to the dead?

Pirates of the Caribbean

The Curse of the Black Pearl

Elizabeth lives on a Caribbean island, a very dangerous place. A young blacksmith is interested in her, but pirates are interested, too. Where do the pirates come from and what do they want? Is there really a curse on their ship? And why can't they enjoy their gold?

There are hundreds of Penguin Readers to choose from – world classics, film adaptations, modern-day crime and adventure, short stories, biographies, American classics, non-fiction, plays ...

For a complete list of all Penguin Readers titles, please contact your local Pearson Longman office or visit our website.